Money
Then and Now

Antonio Sacre, M.A.

Reader Consultants

Brian Allman, M.A.
Classroom Teacher, West Virginia

Cheryl Norman Lane, M.A.Ed.
Classroom Teacher
Chino Valley Unified School District

iCivics Consultants

Emma Humphries, Ph.D.
Chief Education Officer

Taylor Davis, M.T.
Director of Curriculum and Content

Natacha Scott, MAT
Director of Educator Engagement

Publishing Credits

Rachelle Cracchiolo, M.S.Ed., *Publisher*
Emily R. Smith, M.A.Ed., *VP of Content Development*
Véronique Bos, *Creative Director*
Dani Neiley, *Associate Editor*
Fabiola Sepulveda, *Series Designer*
Ana Sebastian, Illustrator, pages 6–9

Image Credits: p4 Shutterstock/Primakov; p10 Alamy/www.BibleLandPictures.com; p11 Getty Images/UniversalImagesGroup; p13 Library of Congress [LC-DIG-pga-08593]; p16 Alamy/The Picture Art Collection; p18 Shutterstock/Anthony Hall; p21 top Library of Congress [HABS PA-1011]; p23 Getty Images/Carsten/Stringer; p29 Library of Congress [LC-USF34-050079-E]; all other images from iStock and/or Shutterstock

TCM Teacher Created Materials
5482 Argosy Avenue
Huntington Beach, CA 92649
www.tcmpub.com

ISBN 978-1-0876-1553-0

Table of Contents

Would You Rather...?

Why is money important? Who invented money? How has it changed over time, especially in the United States? Could people ever live without money?

Speaking of money, would you rather have one hundred thirty quarters or one twenty-dollar bill? Would you rather have five thousand dollars or one bitcoin? Before answering these and other questions, let's look at how people got the things they needed before money was invented.

When early humans unlocked the secrets of agriculture and taming animals, people paid for what they needed by **bartering**. Let's say a wheat farmer wanted to trade some wheat for a cow. How much wheat equals one cow? People had different answers to this question.

Money made these transactions easier. Money was portable, durable, and convenient. You could pay a handful of coins for three chickens. The chicken farmer could give those coins to a dairy farmer for five gallons of milk. Easy? Not so easy. Who says what the coins are worth? Where does the U.S. government fit in to all this?

Jump into Fiction

A Skateboard for a Bike?

Stella was putting the finishing touches on an elaborate replica of Independence Hall for her science project when her mom knocked on her door. She came into the room holding a cell phone.

"Wow, you've been working incredibly hard on your project!" her mom exclaimed.

"Thanks, Mom! What's up?" Stella asked.

"Mario's dad asked to put you on a video call with Mario. He has a problem with his Mars Rover model. Is now good?"

"Sure. Thanks, Mom." Taking the phone, Stella said to her friend, "¿*Hola*, Mario. *Cómo estás*?"

Mario sulked on the small screen and whined, "Miserable, Stella. My rover won't rove! I have to debug all 124 lines of code. Did you figure out how to power the LED bulbs in your hall using produce?"

"Yes, I discovered that citrus provides the longest power," Stella told him.

"Wow! If I can fix my code, maybe we can both place in the district science fair!" Mario said.

Stella sighed happily, "I hope so! I'd love to win that skateboard!"

Mario nodded. "And I'd love to win that bike!"

At the fair, Stella won first place—a bike worth $75! And Mario took second, a skateboard worth $50.

After collecting their prizes, they looked at each other. Stella asked, "Are you thinking what I'm thinking?"

Mario said, "I think I am! I'll give you the skateboard, and you give me the bike! But wait a minute . . . that's not a fair exchange. Your prize is worth $75, and my prize is worth $50."

Stella held the bicycle by the handlebars and murmured, "It's OK. We both created great projects, and we're both getting what we wanted." She rolled the bicycle toward Mario. He set the skateboard on the floor and pushed it to Stella.

Mario stared at the gleaming bicycle, scratched his head thoughtfully, and said, "Well, I could give you something to make up the difference. What about some of my trading cards? I could give you four blocker cards and ten attacker bird cards. That would be worth exactly $25!"

Stella shook her head and said, "No, thanks. I never got into that trading game."

Mario thought some more. "What about that enormous stuffed animal I won at the amusement park?"

"It won't fit in my room," Stella replied.

Mario slapped his head and yelled, "Now, I've got it! How about I give you the $25 I was saving for a new bike?"

Stella smiled. "Wow, thanks! Now we're really equal."

"It's a deal!" Mario said with a big grin.

Back to Nonfiction

Money Since Colonial Times

In the 1600s, European **colonists** were settling across North America. People from France, Spain, and England began to live in what is now the eastern United States. This land was already occupied by American Indians. At first, these colonies were supported by their home countries.

This was especially true for the British colonies. When they needed food, clothing, and tools, ships from England would bring supplies to the colonists. Eventually, the colonists became more self-sufficient. They grew their own food after learning from the American Indians about what crops were best to plant. They made their own clothes and tools. They traded their **surplus** goods with England. England paid for these goods with British gold and silver coins. The colonists used most of this money to buy more British goods they could not make themselves.

The Earliest Money

Money dates back thousands of years. History has record of a coin known as a *shekel* being used in Mesopotamia 5,000 years ago. This coin with a roaring lion on it is from 2,000 years ago. It was found in Turkey. China had money as early as the 600s. And around 1661, the first **banknotes** were used in Europe.

European colonists bringing supplies and boarding ships to North America

This meant there was little money in the colonies. The main way colonists got their necessities was by bartering. This was complicated. Settlers made up other ways of paying for goods. They tried using wampum, or shell beads that they had gotten from trading with American Indians. But this was not allowed by the British. The colonists needed another way to pay for goods.

A New Nation with New Money

The colonists began to use various objects as money. They used tobacco leaves, beaver skins, and Spanish coins to buy goods. Soon, each of the colonies began printing their own money. This made buying and selling goods easier.

England's government forced the colonists to buy certain things only from them. They also taxed many things. This felt unfair to the colonists. These factors, along with the fact that colonists could not have a say in how laws were made, led to a revolution.

The American Revolution ended British control of the colonies. A new country, the United States of America, was formed. The war had lasted for eight years and cost a lot of money. The new country did not want to use taxes to pay for the war. It needed to find other ways to cover the costs of the war. One way the country paid for this was by printing more paper money. These bills were called *continentals*. They printed so many of them that **hyperinflation** occurred. Prices of goods rose in a short amount of time. Another way they paid for the war was by borrowing money from other countries.

This banknote is from 1776.

Colonists dressed as American Indians throw chests of tea into Boston Harbor.

The Boston Tea Party

Before the war, colonists were unhappy with the government. So, they staged protests. One famous protest was the Boston Tea Party. On December 16, 1773, colonists dumped 342 chests of tea into Boston Harbor. They were angry because they were being taxed unfairly.

The Gold Rush and the Civil War

In the mid-1800s, gold was discovered in the West. Many people moved to the area from all over the world. They wanted to mine for gold, hoping they would strike it rich. This led to a **boom** in business. California became a state in 1850 after the increase in population created a need for a structured system of government. The gold rush helped the United States as well. It led to growth in manufacturing, agriculture, and retail across the country. It also led to big changes in transportation. The first cross-country railroad was built in the mid-1800s. Its final stop was in San Francisco.

At the same time, the country was divided over slavery. In the South, plantation owners forced enslaved people to pick crops, such as cotton. Cotton became the most **exported** good for the United States. It was a big factor in the growth of the country. Some states had ended slavery. But some states still wanted to allow slavery. This caused a war.

The Cotton Gin

After cotton is picked, the seeds must be removed. This is a difficult job! Eli Whitney created a machine to help. The cotton gin (right) removed seeds from the fiber. Cotton production in the United States boomed after this invention. It changed the cotton industry. More cotton could be processed on a quicker and larger scale, which boosted the economy.

The Civil War was extremely expensive for the country. The **national debt** grew from $65 million to $2.6 billion. The government needed ways to pay for the war. In 1863, President Abraham Lincoln signed the National Currency Act. This act provided for a national banking system. It also created a national system of paper money and coins. In 1864, it was amended and became known as the National Bank Act.

a Civil War battle in 1862

World War II

The twentieth century saw great changes in much of American life. Slavery had ended. The expansion of the nation continued into the 1900s. Women finally had the right to vote. Many people moved from farms to cities. Millions of people from around the world came to live in America.

Then, a worldwide **economic depression** happened. Many people around the world lost money. The economies of many countries struggled. This was one of the factors that contributed to the start of a global war. World War II cost many lives. It ruined countries. The United States spent billions of dollars during the war.

Rosie the Riveter

A lot of men were drafted into World War II. But people were still needed to work in factories. Women from the middle and working classes were recruited to work in factories. Rosie the Riveter became an icon for these working women. There are two popular drawings associated with Rosie.

Factories had to produce goods, such as tanks, that could be used for the war.

The government asked for people to pay for the war with higher taxes. A wave of patriotism led people all over the country to buy **savings bonds** to fund the war. During the war, many jobs were created so factories could build items needed for the fight. Economically, the United States was better off after the war than it was before.

The Internet and Smartphones

The first computer was invented in the 1940s. There was a boom of people buying personal computers in the 1980s. The internet was also invented during this time. It was originally made for the military. It became available for public use by the 1990s. Every year, computers have gotten faster. They have become more powerful. There are more and more ways to use them.

For example, people can create and sell goods with the help of computers. Then, they can send their items to producers around the world. Producers make the items. Customers order the items. And delivery companies bring the items right to customers' doors.

Early phones and computers look very different from ones you see today!

People can use their cell phones to pay in stores.

Cell phones that can access the internet have been around since 1996. They became popular in the early 2000s. Now, half of the people in the world own smartphones. People can reach one another almost instantly. Smartphones get more powerful each year, too.

Technology has created a lot of economic changes over the years. You can use an app to get a ride somewhere. You can buy your groceries online. And you can access your **bank account** through a website or an app. Advancements in technology have created many new opportunities and possibilities.

Technology and the Economy

Technology is a key factor in influencing economic growth. Advancements in technology mean that more goods and services can be produced, which boosts the economy. Most of the richest people in the world are involved in technology companies!

Cash, Checks, Credit, and Crypto

When early humans would hunt, gather, grow, or make things they needed, there was no need for money. When they could not get what they needed, they bartered. Once bartering became difficult, money was invented. Items such as metal coins, shells, animal skins, and eventually paper had set values and were exchanged for goods and services.

At first, people kept their money with them or stored it in their homes. But what would happen if it were lost or burned in a fire? What if someone stole it from them? The money would be gone, and the hard work it took to earn that money would be for nothing. People had to find a solution. One solution to this problem was banks. Banks were created so people could have places to store their money safely. When people got paid, they took the coins or paper bills to a bank. They deposited the money into their accounts at the bank. Then, the bank kept that money in a vault. Whenever people wanted their money, they went to the bank and asked for it.

First National Bank in Philadelphia in the early 1900s

The First Bank

The oldest bank still in existence is *Banca Monte dei Paschi di Siena* in Siena, Italy. It was opened in 1624. This bank traces its roots to 1492.

Checks and Credit Cards

As the population grew, banks in the United States could not keep all the deposits in one place. They moved much of the money to central banks. They kept records of what each person had deposited.

Checks are slips of paper that people write on so they can transfer money into and out of their accounts. People first started using printed checks in the 1700s. People could also take their checks to the banks. The banks would exchange checks for cash.

But there were problems with checks. In the 1800s, there were many banks in the United States. There was no good system to see if the banks had the money in their accounts. Some people **forged** checks. When a shopper wanted to pay for something with a check, the store needed to determine whether the bank even existed. The person had to prove they owned the account.

In 1950, the **credit card** was invented to make it easier for people to buy things. People could charge their cards and pay the bills once a month. By 1958, some credit cards allowed you to carry a balance between months. The balance is the amount of money you owe to the credit card company. Those early cards are exactly like our credit cards today.

Fees, Fees, and More Fees

Many companies charge fees each time a credit card is used at a store. The store usually pays these fees. But some companies charge customers fees for using their credit cards. In 2018, consumers paid more than $100 billion in fees to credit card companies.

A customer pays with his credit card in 1955.

Digital Payments

By the early 2000s, people were widely using the internet. Soon, people were able to use the internet to pay for things. People started paying their bills online instead of writing checks.

This led to a new kind of business, one that focused on securing online payments. Many people did not want to share their banking information online. These companies found ways to keep this information safe. Customers felt safer paying for things this way. In the 2000s, people often chose to shop on their computers. They stopped going to stores as often. They had their goods delivered to their homes. They no longer had to buy only what the local stores had on their shelves. They could buy anything the internet-connected world had to offer.

Companies have also found ways for people to quickly and easily pay using their smartphones. **Digital wallets** were invented. These systems hold money and credit cards like physical wallets do. Banking information is safely stored in the online system.

Over time, fraud has become a problem. In an increasingly digital world, criminals have learned how to steal personal information online. In some cases, they open accounts in other people's names. Or they **hack** into accounts. They use computers to guess people's passwords. This is called *identity theft*. This has resulted in billions of dollars of stolen money.

Think and Talk

What are the benefits and downsides of digital payments?

Technology allows people to make easier and faster payments.

Debit versus Credit

A **debit card** is linked to money held in a bank account. You can spend as much as you have in the account. Debit cards offer the same protections credit cards do. A credit card is linked to a credit limit, so even if you do not have the money in a bank account, you can spend up to the limit. But be careful! If you do not pay the bill when it is due, you will have to pay **interest**.

Cryptocurrency

Some money only exists digitally. This is known as **cryptocurrency**. Bitcoin is the most popular cryptocurrency. It was invented in 2009.

When you have bitcoin, you do not have to visit a bank to access, use, or withdraw your money. Instead, people who own this type of currency can send it directly to one another using the internet. They use digital wallets instead of physical bills and coins. People access their digital wallets through the internet.

A cryptocurrency wallet allows a person to view and manage their money.

Bitcoin ATMs allow users to buy and sell bitcoin.

Each transaction is connected to the others using **cryptography**. This is how the system stays secure. There are many codes that protect the entire system. Every person has their own private key or code. Think of it like your fingerprint: it is unique to you. People use their private keys to access their money. They also have public keys, which is how they can send money to others. It is extremely difficult to hack these accounts and fake records.

People can buy bitcoin themselves, or they can make bitcoin. Making a bitcoin on a computer is called *mining*. You need powerful computers, lots of electricity, and a lot of knowledge to do this!

Journey through Time

The creation of money made it easier for people to get the things they needed. In the United States, how money has changed has had a lot to do with the events that shaped the nation. It's hard to talk about money without talking about history!

Every person has a say in how their money is used. You can spend your money, or you can save your money. You affect what happens to that money. You might buy something at a store or online. Your purchase affects how companies think about spending their money. They may want to produce more or less of something, depending on supply and demand.

Humans have always had to figure out how to get the things they need. They had to figure out how to make money work. They had to figure out how to protect it. Each generation uses what they have available and tries to make the best decisions they can. And with new technology comes new decisions. What are the benefits? What are the costs? Are there better ways to get it accomplished? From bartering to mining cryptocurrency, how people use money has changed over time.

Think and Talk

How do you think people will use money in the future?

WINGS
TRI-ME
Spaghetti

Glossary

bank account—an account at a bank where a person can withdraw and deposit money

banknotes—pieces of paper money

bartering—trading goods and services without using money

boom—a period of increased business activity that makes many people more money

colonists—settlers or inhabitants of a place under the control of another country

credit card—a card that allows a buyer to buy something up to a certain limit, without having the money in their account at the time

cryptocurrency—a digital currency developed through code

cryptography—the practice of encoding (scrambling) and decoding (solving) of information

debit card—a card that allows a buyer to transfer money from their account to a merchant

digital wallets—software-based systems on smartphones that allow people to store payment information and make transactions

economic depression—a time in which business activity goes down and there is less money, goods, and services

exported—sent to be sold in another country

forged—made something with the intention of it being fake or false

hack—to gain illegal access

hyperinflation—extreme increase in the price of goods and services, often caused by an increase in volume of printed money

interest—a charge for borrowed money that the borrower has to pay back

national debt—the total amount of money that a country's government owes to other countries, companies, etc.

savings bonds—pieces of paper issued by a government in exchange for money from the public to pay for something the public needs, with the promise to be paid back with interest

surplus—an outstanding amount

Index

5000 0000 0000 000
5000
MONTH/YEAR
VALID THRU 11/19
MR. CARDHOLDER

Civics in Action

Money can be confusing. It comes in many different forms. Each form has to be used in certain ways. Many students know little about money. But you can change that! You can teach them all about the different types of money and ways to use money.

1. Decide on topics to include (paper money, checks, credit cards, bitcoin, etc.).
2. Gather information from the book and online.
3. Create a mini-encyclopedia of money for kids.
4. Share your work!